Unfolded

Brian Schubring
&
Linda Schubring

Unfolded

Lessons *in* Transformation
from an Origami Crane

WILEY

Published by John Wiley & Sons, Inc., Hoboken, New Jersey.
Published simultaneously in Canada.

For general information on our other products and services or for technical support, please contact our Customer Care Department within the United States at (800) 762-2974, outside the United States at (317) 572-3993 or fax (317) 572-4002.

Wiley also publishes its books in a variety of electronic formats. Some content that appears in print may not be available in electronic formats. For more information about Wiley products, visit our web site at www.wiley.com.

Library of Congress Cataloging-in-Publication Data is Available:

ISBN: 9781394338092 (cloth)
ISBN: 9781394338108 (ePub)
ISBN: 9781394338115 (ePDF)

Cover Design: Wiley
Cover Image: © Prostock-studio/Adobe Stock
Author Photos: © Scott Rokis
SKY10103301_041125

To our loving parents, Wayne & Diane
and Don & Marlene

Who nurtured us to live our dreams

To our daughter, Camila, and nephews, Conor
and Weston, whose dreams are unfolding

We are cheering for you

Contents

Believe in your dreams with hope and courage
Your reshaping and transformation are not to be feared

One's true self is found within, waiting for its discovery
Embrace your journey of acceptance
Unfold the potential of your dreams
With confidence take flight

Trust in yourself, you will become free to try
In a world of possibilities, why not fly?

Foreword

In my roles as Chief Information Security Officer and Chief Information Officer, it was always a top priority to ensure that my teams operated at their highest potential. I needed teams that were not only skilled and knowledgeable but also engaged, empowered, and united in purpose. Individuals had to feel seen, heard, and valued, while also being motivated to support one another and work collaboratively toward a common goal.

One of the most profound lessons I've learned throughout my career is that building a team isn't just about hiring talented individuals; it's about creating an environment where each person's unique strengths are understood, appreciated, and strategically applied. My ability to cultivate such environments can be traced directly back to my work with Dr. Linda and Brian Schubring.

I met Linda and Brian over a decade ago during a career transition. In a previous role, I had built a strong team from the ground up—hiring exceptional talent, mentoring them, and encouraging their growth. However, when I moved on to a new position, I realized that while the team had thrived under my leadership, it wasn't a *team* in the truest sense. It had been held together by the strength of my presence. Once I left, many of the individuals I had developed also moved on. It was a humbling realization and one that led to a promise: I would never again build a group of individuals who relied solely on a leader for cohesion. I would focus on building teams that were equipped to thrive together, even in my absence.

That's where Linda and Brian's expertise came in. They introduced me to a powerful system grounded in their deep understanding of psychology, human behavior, and individual strengths. Through their guidance, I learned how to identify and appreciate the unique wiring of each team member. They provided a shared language to talk about those differences and taught us how to apply this understanding to foster respect, trust, and collaboration. Their work didn't just transform our approach to teamwork—it transformed us as individuals personally and professionally.

Linda and Brian have continued to refine their approach, working with tens of thousands of people, learning from their experiences, and continually evolving their methods. Their belief in the potential of every individual—to grow, learn, and change—remains unwavering. Their techniques are not about labeling or rigid definitions of "right" or "wrong," but about meeting each person where they are, with compassion, and helping them see new possibilities. There is no judgment—only a commitment to growth, self-awareness, and the belief that we all have the power to continually remake ourselves.

Unfolded is the culmination of Linda and Brian's life's work—a reflection of their ongoing learning and growth. An unfolding and refolding of their personal maps. The characters in this allegory embody the full spectrum of human traits, and as Linda points out, we all likely embody these traits to some degree. Each character is essential to the balance, just as each member is essential to the success of a team.

In a world filled with uncertainty and challenge, *Unfolded* invites us to imagine what might be possible if we gave ourselves permission to never stop growing. It reminds us that we are stronger than we often think, that the answers we seek are often already within us, and that, most importantly, we live in a world where we must support one another and be open to receiving support in return.

This book is a gift—a blueprint for growth, both personal and collective—and I am honored to share it with you.

Deborah Dixson
Retired Global Chief Information
Security Officer, Best Buy
Current Coach and Mentor

Introduction by Linda

Unfolded is an allegory for individuals or teams with a dream: a dream to uncover a new dream or a new identity. The world needs people and leaders with the courage to dream new dreams big enough to reach the world and bright enough to heal it. *Unfolded* points to our life's work separately and together as business partners and partners in marriage.

One day at our kitchen table, Brian slid two typed pages across to me. I read his words and was moved. In a few paragraphs, he baited me. I knew he was onto something. Brian found a way to articulate why we do the important work of listening to and inspiring others to embrace who they are and dream into their greatest potential. Most people know change is inevitable, so what happens when we are changing from the inside out?

Brian's idea of the journey of an origami crane he named OC began to unfold as he shared his words.

His dream took flight with an origami crane, some other origami animals, and some guides. Brian's dream took form in the context of an actual city playground near our home. It was beneath the shade of the cottonwood trees that Brian's idea was birthed. I joined him in writing the allegory in pursuit of our dream to deepen our impact and further our reach to help people grow. We've taken turns breathing life into these words because this story maps to our lived experience.

Unfolded represents our own ups and downs of our journey. We are students of our own story. In each place of growth, transition, or pivot, we looked around and saw a cast of characters. We can name the people and places who shaped us as kids, young people, and adults. Both Brian's and my journeys involved leading people, being on stages, and catalyzing movements.

Then our stories intersected both personally and professionally. As a married couple, we could tell you more about the community during my cancer battle, who was there in my doctoral pursuits, our injuries, failures, triumphs, and our travels around the world that helped us expand and focus our work with people. As individuals we've each had our own stories of unfolding and reshaping our lives.

Introduction by Linda

Unfolded gives a nod to many of our clients in each season of our business and the leaders who have trusted us with their people. *Unfolded* represents how Brian and I create space between us for people to accept themselves, learn to flourish, and have some fun. We believe the journey of growth begins with reflection in order to make more meaningful moves. In the tens of thousands of people we have worked with one thing became clear: Brian and I seek to transform how leaders express their brilliance and beauty for the benefit of humanity.

The book begins with a **Prelude by Brian**. You will read the genesis of this work and the soul behind the idea. I invite you to read the Prelude, to get a glimpse of the Brian I see.

The five chapters tell the story of the Origami Crane named OC, who had a dream and went after it. Chapter 1, Dream, begins with OC's dream to fly. Chapter 2, Play, grounds the dream in practice disguised as play. Chapter 3, Try, describes the intentional practice in OC's attempts to fly, failures, and the need for unlearning to learn. Chapter 4, Fly, describes the flight and what can be learned when we soar. Chapter 5, Home, is where the invitation is to reflect and share.

Maybe the allegory is enough for you. Read it and enjoy. Don't let us interrupt your imagination or self-reflection. However, if you want to keep going, the final section has more handles for your thinking, feeling, acting, and reacting. Brian and I wrote the **Reflection and Application** together to inspire you to track your stories and dreams to components of the *Unfolded* story. This section has prompts and encouragement helpful to you or your teams or communities.

Finally, in the **Postlude by Linda**, I offer some concluding thoughts, but OC gets the last word in a **Meditation**. Our hope is that you'll try. Our dream is that you'll fly.

Prelude by Brian

Have you ever had a dream you wished would come true?

Have you ever dreamed a dream that helped pull you through?

Are you pursuing a dream that feels the most you?

Are you waiting for a dream to land in your queue?

At times there is a need to remember a dream, to reimagine a dream, or to let a dream go. Sometimes it's time to dream a new dream, to inspire others to dream, or to help someone else make their dream a reality. When dreams unfold, clues about your greatest potential lie in the creases.

As a young boy, I had a dream that someday I would fly.

My earliest memories in childhood are of watching airplanes take off, land, and fly across the sky. My dream of flight was fueled by what I could see and that our family home was located beneath the flight paths near the Minneapolis-St. Paul International Airport. We were close enough to hear the roar of the jet engines as planes took off and then came the metallic whir as they soared directly over our house. The regular noise and vibrations stirred a desire in me that maybe someday I could fly a plane.

I guess I have had many dreams.

When I unfolded my dream of flying, some of the clues in the creases is that I am a dreamer. There are dreams in my childhood where I imagined being a professional hockey player, a lifeguard, a pilot, and even a doctor. Most times, I just dreamed that we'd move to a bigger house so I would have my own bedroom. Each of these childhood dreams were directly influenced by the place I grew up, the people surrounding me, and the opportunities afforded me. My dreams have inspired me my entire life.

Of all my childhood dreams I was shaped most by two dreams: to become a professional hockey player and to fly an airplane. The first dream ended in injury by the age of 20 when I scored my last goal with a third-degree shoulder separation with torn ligaments. Letting go of that dream was both physically and mentally crushing. The second dream I fulfilled by the age of five. Maybe I peaked too early, but fulfilling that dream gave birth to a life of dreams.

As a little boy in the 1970s, I collected Hot Wheels cars and kept them in the accompanying car briefcase for a garage. I also collected die-cast planes and kept those in a shoebox. I had enough planes to play "airport" and my favorite plane was a military green fighter jet. I even built planes out of Legos, and I impatiently glued model planes whenever I had a chance.

To know my dad is to know a father who would get on the floor of our family room and jump into the fun of the game of "airport." He let my imagination grow. Looking back, my father fueled my dream to fly.

By five years old, my dad was stoking my dream. He would talk about airplanes with me, how they could fly, the aerodynamics, and taught me to identify which type of aircraft flew over our neighborhood. My dad would even take the family on adventures near the airport. We'd park along the service road that ran alongside the runway to sit and watch airplanes take off and land. This experience was thrilling but was not a key factor in fulfilling my dream.

My dad had a private pilot's license. One of my father's dreams was to fly planes and to become a commercial pilot. His dream to fly planes came true, but the commercial pilot part did not.

My dad's dream to fly commercially coincided with the time in history when the Korean War ended and pilots who had flown thousands of hours were back home and looking for jobs. Forever buoyant, my dad pivoted from his dream. He and three friends shared ownership of a Cessna 183. My dad earned his pilot's license and made good use of his time in flight. Some of my best memories and my mom's more terrifying memories are from the family time in the little plane.

My dad didn't just take me on rides. My father taught me the fundamentals of flying. He taught me the importance of a pre-flight walk around. Dad showed me what to look at on the wings, fuselage, and landing gear. He taught me what to pull on and move, and how to start the plane. My dad taught me how to read the basic instruments and how to use the yoke to actually maneuver the plane while in flight.

One day, my dad and I went for a flight, just the two of us. Prior to the flight, we did our routines, took off, and were soon soaring across the sky. I watched with wonder as the world below us passed slowly by. I watched the instruments moving, and

Prelude by Brian

my dad's steady hand at the controls. Then my dad turned to me and said, "Son, take us home."

I asked my dad to recount this story on a summer's day 52 years later while we were at my nephew's golf tournament. As my dad recalls the story, "You immediately took control of the yoke which looked like half of a steering wheel, turned the plane around, and flew us back to the airport."

I asked, "How old was I?"

My dad replied, "Five."

Laughing, I asked, "Dad, you trusted me to fly the plane at that age?"

His reaction was immediate and sure, "Well, you always had a good sense of direction. And I knew you could do it."

It took me a moment to process this whole scenario as a father myself, and then I asked, "How far did you let me fly? I obviously did not land the plane."

My dad replied, "Oh, I don't know. Maybe around 1,000 feet I took the controls back and landed. You weren't ready for that yet."

My dream to fly: fulfilled at age five.

Prelude by Brian

If you believe in anything
Believe in you
Believe in your beauty and brilliance
Believe in your potential and possibility
Believe in your light, your life, your love
If you believe in something
Believe you can fly!

Prelude by Brian

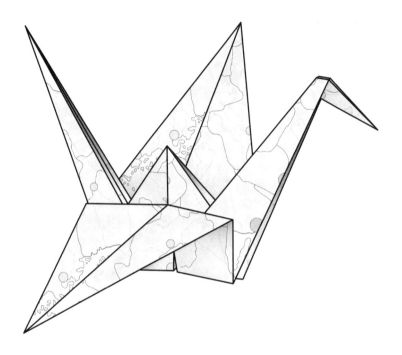

There once was an origami crane who dreamed of becoming a paper plane. The origami crane, named OC, lived in a city playground located beneath two great cottonwood trees.

OC grew up with other origami animals who had been folded and placed in the playground by many pairs of colorful hands.

The colorful hands work above the clouds where the sun shines brighter. These hands work tirelessly at a table preparing their creations for the land below. Before a shape is formed, the colorful hands choose their paper. Some of the paper is large and other sheets are small. The papers have patterns and designs that look like flowers, musical notes, or maps. Some papers are bright. Other patterns are muted. Some paper almost begs to be folded while other paper resists even the slightest bend. All paper squares have a story to tell.

Music and laughter fill the table as the colorful hands do their folding and creasing. The first few folds are the valley folds and mountain folds, which are basic to every origami animal. The creases guide the next fold. Some hands move quickly and other hands more slowly. Some hands use tools to make intricate impressions, while other hands methodically press the folds into place.

Sometimes though, the table is more subdued. The colorful hands cringe when the fold isn't perfect or bent a little too much. The table above the clouds falls quiet when a fragile paper tears.

Still, the colorful hands take care to form the origami animals into distinct shapes with unique voices. Dreams are breathed into the origami creations with every crease and fold. As each of the animals becomes more recognizable, the excitement grows.

The table of colorful hands responds to each origami creation: a slow and methodical exhale with Turtle's last fold, the wow and wonder about OC's courage, the giggles about what Young Crane (YC) will mean to the world, and the hope and unspoken questions around the active Rabbit. The colorful hands remember the exquisite elegance of the folding of Owl and the integrity of releasing Eagle to soar. No one really talks about Fox.

··· ⟨🦉⟩ ···

Owl was on watch in the city playground beneath the cottonwood trees waiting for the new origami animals to be placed in the playground. Word came from above the clouds that the colorful hands were almost done with their latest creations.

Owl looked with appreciation at his geometric folds that have both a worn and regal look. If his map could talk, it would tell of a life well lived and many lessons learned. His map included great loss in the valleys and awe in the mountain top highs. If his map could talk, it would give an account of ordinary days and extraordinary joys. Owl knew the importance of being made of a map, for it provided him with all the clarity and confidence he ever needed for his life's path.

Owl remembered the unique folds in his life, and the parts of his map no one sees. He thanked the creases of his life and even embraced the crumples. He delighted most in the people and places represented on his map. Word from above the clouds indicated he might have a new favorite this time around. Owl wondered what form and shape he might see, and what type of map they might be.

··· ···

When folded and ready, the colorful hands joyfully release the animals. Some animals go to places along the water, other animals are placed in the country-side, and OC and her origami friends were placed in the playground in the city. They grew together in a playground that had three developmental sections for the youngest, young, and older animals to play.

OC was shaped as much by the colorful hands as the friends of all ages in the city playground. Of all the friends, OC's playful spirit stirred joy when she leaned into her dreams. Maybe OC's origami friends had dreams too, but OC knew at an early age that if her dream would come true, she would need help from her friends.

Intuitively OC knew that she couldn't achieve it alone. Her friends included her origami friends: Turtle, Young Crane (YC), Rabbit, and Fox; a golden retriever puppy named Golden; and a compassionate and courageous origami guide named Owl. The playground offered a place for all the friends to grow.

One day something caught OC's attention. OC looked up at the sky and dreamed of soaring like the birds and planes she saw passing overhead. She wondered if she could ever fly as high as the feathered birds or as far as the shiny planes. OC dreamed of flying. This dream was deep within her. Even as an origami crane, she knew that one day she would fly.

To fly, she had to try. And through her trying she would one day fulfill her dream.

For this dream I hold
Is loving and bold
The dream is so close
It's just beneath the fold

Unfolded

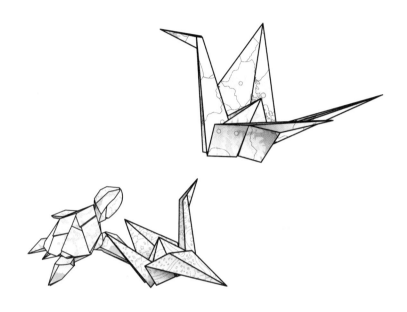

"Wait up!"
"No fair."
"Faster!"

OC chuckled recounting her early years in the small playground among the other origami animals. They were all practicing using their voices. Eventually they found what fit for each of them.

In the first days, OC was so excited to be in this new place which seemed so large with many things to do and many places to explore. OC saw folded animals just like her playing together. They encouraged OC to join them in their imaginative games.

In this small playground, there were little swings, low platforms, and sand toys. There were benches all around this area for those who would sit and watch the animals play. The ground was made of soft rubber, surrounded by sand, to protect the youngest when they stumbled and fell. Here the animals began to build their friendships with each other. Here there was a sense of safety while they played. The playground was a place to try new things, meet new friends, and a place of practice and having fun. Nothing in this part of the playground was too high or too challenging.

OC's favorite friend was Turtle. Turtle was encouraging and playful. Turtle was gentle with his words and thoughtful in the ways he played with OC. Over time, Turtle would help OC get to know the other animals and together they played games that would inspire greater imagination, growth, and a sense of belonging.

OC continued to deepen her friendships during these early years: playing in the sand, laughing, and learning how to share. Rabbit was OC's fun friend, who was one of the first to react to whatever was going on and first to join in whatever the activity was. As the most extroverted and up-in-everyone's-business friend, Rabbit would speak her thoughts aloud. Her voice would only become louder.

9

Young Crane, nicknamed YC, was OC's younger brother and closest friend. YC was energetic and positive. YC was smaller than the rest, but his joyful heart carried the most optimism. He played on the small playground too, but often in OC's shadow.

There were plenty of bumps and bruises on the little playground, but OC's friends were there to pick each other up and encourage each other. Well, except for her friend Fox.

Fox was an interesting and prickly friend. Fox was ever present on the playground, even though you did not know where he was all the time. Fox would hide under the swings and scare the friends and laugh at them. At other times, Fox would play with the older animals or be a loner in the rose garden. Whenever Fox was around, the animals were a little on edge.

Unfolded

Fox would play in the games the other animals were playing, and he was also quick to judge, yelping or criticizing in disapproval. Fox acted like he was better than everyone else. He was quick to confront those who were trying to stand out or try something new. Even with his harsh voice, Fox was a part of the playground and all that made this young group of friends who they were.

OC was a beautiful crane, with a long neck and tail, two broad wings, and a sleek body. She accepted her shape and form, believing that, because she had wings, she was meant to fly and to explore the world beyond the playground where she found herself. Her voice was yet to be discovered. OC didn't always have words for the dreams she tucked in her heart.

OC's belief in flying was encouraged and inspired by seeing the graceful and easy movement of the feathered birds in the cottonwood trees. The brightly feathered birds were all different sizes and a variety of colors. They flew beyond the trees, hopped from branch to branch, chased one another, and sometimes rested within the shade of the leaves. As OC watched the feathered birds in the cottonwoods, she believed one day she might fly.

Her wise friend, Owl, kept her focused. Owl asked, "What do you see?"

OC replied, "I see myself in flight. But I am just an origami crane."

Owl looked her in the eyes and asked, "Why not fly?"

OC wondered, and answered, "But I do not know how."

Owl replied with great kindness, "If you want to fly, you need to try."

OC responded to Owl, "I will probably never fly like birds in the branches of the cottonwood trees."

Owl asked, "Do you believe you can fly? If you want to fly, you have to try."

Do you believe you can fly? If you want to fly, you have to try.

By watching the birds above, OC imagined how she could fly like the feathered birds. Noticing the bright colors of these birds, OC wondered if she too would one day change color, or if she would grow bigger, or simply what she might look like when she grew older. Maybe then she would be able to fly.

OC felt wonder and happiness watching the birds playing in the branches. Even though OC did not understand how to be like them, looking at her shape as a crane, she did not know how she could actually fly. Through Owl's nudge, OC was inspired to create a game to play, and that game was called *Fly*.

And with those few words, OC began to imagine what it would be like to fly. She began to try.

While everyone else was playing, OC would sneak behind the trunk of the cottonwood tree and pretend to be in the branches above. She guessed she would settle for playing on the ground. She would try to leap from exposed root to root. The first leaps looked more like awkward tumbling and stumbling. OC felt the sand in her folds when she'd trip. OC quickly learned that she really didn't have what it took to fly and began to doubt her dream. She didn't have feathers after all.

As determined children are, OC's dreams didn't die easily and she kept tumbling. OC would playfully sing in her mind on repeat, "I'm flying. I'm flying. I'm in flight."

Each day, OC snuck off and played *Fly* by herself just long enough so the other friends wouldn't miss her. She'd return to whatever else was happening on the playground. No one really asked about the dust on her form, not even Fox.

One day, when OC was jumping from exposed root to root, she was so lost in her game her inside voice turned into her outside voice. She repeated the made-up singsong with glee because she was free. OC didn't see Turtle who had moseyed up to the tree trunk.

"Hi OC. You're what? I wanna play," Turtle said.

OC froze and felt found out even though it was just Turtle, her most trusted friend. OC felt herself blush. At least it wasn't Fox who exposed her.

Trying to recover, OC lied, "Hi Turtle. I'm just checking out the roots by the tree."

Unfolded

Turtle kept his gaze steady. "But I heard you were flying. I wanna play."

OC knew Turtle was safe, but now someone else knew what OC feared the whole time: she really didn't have what it took to fly.

OC pushed back her doubt and fear and said, "Fine. Wanna play *Fly?*"

Turtle nodded and suggested, "Yes, and maybe we could play over there with everyone else."

Turtle turned and made his way back to the platform where everyone else was playing.

OC wondered what she had done. She brushed herself off and followed Turtle.

··· ···

Turtle announced to the friends that OC had a good idea of a game.

"Let me show you. This is how you play," OC said. And she started making it up as she went.

She would jump up on the low platform, and look over the edge at the sand below and wonder how she could fly off the platform. From the edge, OC would look up and see the feathered birds above. She didn't know quite what to do, but that didn't stop her.

OC moved to the back edge of the small platform as her excitement built. OC told her friends Rabbit, Turtle, YC, and even Fox what she was going to do, and they watched curiously at this new game. Beginning with a short run, she flapped her wings energetically, in hopes that running off the platform would help her fly.

As soon as OC began her run across the platform, Fox leapt to his feet to meet her. He quickly ran to the edge of the platform. With a sudden stop, he faced OC, growled, and blocked her attempt to fly. OC felt instant fear and slid to a stop, coming beak to nose with Fox. Fox sneered, "You will never fly. Why try?"

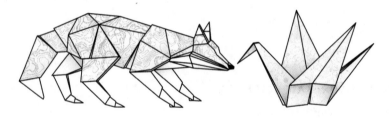

OC slowly backed into the opposite corner of the platform. Her first attempt to fly had failed before it started.

Many attempts to fly followed. OC would run across the platform, approaching the edge at full speed, and then come to a quick stop just before it was time to jump whether Fox was there or not. Although she believed she was meant to fly, self-doubt and fear would arise, causing OC to stop short. Even so, this too-quick start and stop became part of playing the game of *Fly*.

All of OC's friends except her brother YC would play the game of *Fly*, too. YC was just too young at this time. Rabbit and Fox jumped up onto the low platform with excitement, and were the first and fastest to jump off the platform. They seemed to not have much fear and would be the first to compare their play to others.

Rabbit would hop easily off the edge. Fox, laughing, was close behind Rabbit lunging even higher than she. Still laughing, Fox smirked and said, "It's not called *Hop*, Rabbit. It doesn't even matter. You cannot fly anyway. Rabbits don't fly."

But Rabbit kept playing the game.

Over and over the friends would have so much fun playing the new game of *Fly*. OC saw their ease and joy, and tried even harder to fly.

Even Turtle played along, in the unlikely possibility that he too could fly. Mostly, Turtle would walk slowly and intentionally across the platform and toward the edge. Instead of stopping at the edge of the platform, Turtle kept going just like all his friends. Then, he'd simply tumble off and land in the sand below. The first time, Turtle ended up on his back.

Rabbit hopped to help Turtle, but not before Fox arrived. With a sinister laugh, Fox spun Turtle on his shell. OC soon arrived. With Rabbit's help, they stopped Turtle from spinning and turned him right side up again.

Rabbit tried to stay in Fox's good grace, so she laughed and asked Fox, "Did you see what Turtle is trying to do? He was trying to fly, and just fell off the edge of the platform."

Fox said, "Turtles don't fly. We should tell Turtle to stop trying."

Turtle overheard this conversation between Rabbit and Fox and said to them, "Hey, I can play, too! I did not fall off the edge, I flew off the edge just like everyone else."

Fox said to Turtle, "Save your shell, Turtle."

Caught in between friends, Rabbit blurted out "Listen. Turtle, you probably shouldn't play this game anymore. Maybe you can play somewhere else."

Turtle liked the game and continued to play, laughing at his own failed attempts, and encouraging everyone no matter how well they could fly. Fox and Rabbit made *Fly* a competition, but for Turtle, playing together was more important than how far you could jump off the platform.

Unfolded

In this small playground there also lived a golden retriever puppy named Golden. He was there to protect and encourage all the origami animals. Just a small furry puppy, he would often run around the small platform in a circle, often being chased by Fox who occasionally nipped at his tail. Golden's joy and excitement of simply being a puppy gave a little extra boost of confidence to OC. At times that playful puppy stirred the courage for OC to take another small risk or another small flight.

During this time, Rabbit and Fox played together often, and at times finding comfort in watching from the side and not feeling the need to be involved in this game of *Fly* all the time.

Rabbit would ask Fox, "Why does OC think she can fly? She is not that kind of bird. And she is not that good at flying anyway."

Fox, added to the conversation, "OC is trying too hard. She will never fly." Rabbit and Fox laughed.

Rabbit asked, "Fox, do you think she will ever fly like the birds?"

"No." Fox said, "I have never seen an origami crane fly."

Some days when Rabbit and Fox would sit on the platform, they blocked the way for OC to play the game *Fly*. OC noticed them on the platform, and did not really give them a second thought. "I will try to fly further another time," OC thought.

When Fox played along, he would often run off the edge of the platform, easily and confidently jumping over YC and Turtle, then running alongside the puppy as they circled the playground. OC noticed how easy it was for Fox to run and jump, desiring the same ease and enjoyment.

With each new attempt, OC kept trying and trying to fly further. Starting in the corner of the small platform, flapping her wings as much as she could, running as fast as she could, then jumping, reaching, and striving to fly as far as she could. OC enjoyed the play and the practice. YC was proud of his sister, OC, trying to fly and thought to himself, "One day, I will be like my older sister."

The game of *Fly* became more fun and challenging. OC would run and jump off the edge, first over the back of Turtle, then over the top of YC, then landing in the sand awkwardly. One time, OC felt something strange when hitting the sand, she looked to her wing and saw that it was a bit bent. She acted as if everything was ok.

One day, Owl swooped down and said, "I saw you laughing while playing your new game. How are you feeling?"

OC replied, "Yes, playing here is so much fun. My friends are the best, mostly. No matter how hard I try, I simply cannot fly like the birds. I guess that makes me feel sad."

Owl asked, "So you still dream of flying like the birds?"

OC responded, "Yes, I do want to fly higher. But I am afraid I don't know how and will never be able to reach my dream. And what if I fail?"

Owl replied warmly,

> For your dream to grow, you will need to let go.

"For your dream to grow, you will need to let go. You will experience failure, and you will experience success. Each time you try, you will learn, adapt, and try again. If you stay in this playground too long, your dream will be limited by what becomes familiar."

Owl continued, "Reflect on who you are, look within. Everything you need is there. Nothing is missing. And consider what you are made of, you are a map folded by many colorful hands. I will help you learn how to read it and understand what this means for your dream. Remember, you can always trust your map to provide you with the clarity and confidence you need for wherever your life's pathway leads. All your answers are there."

Turtle was close by and overheard this conversation between Owl and OC. He noticed for the first time that both of his friends were made of maps. How had he not seen that before? How incredible to have friends folded so beautifully from map paper. He dared to wonder if he was made of a map, too. Maybe the map was just for the origami with wings like Owl and OC.

On his way back to the sand toys, Turtle stopped by the pond. The wind was still and the sun was at the right angle along the shore. He calmly glanced at his reflection in the water. Was that a map he saw? He saw vast areas of shades of blue, occasional green shapes, light brown lines, and some black words or something that he didn't know how to read.

It turns out that maps aren't just for the ones folded with wings. Turtle was made of a paper map, too, but what did that mean? He would need to think about what he saw for a while.

The friends made so many memories playing in the playground together. Every game taught them something new about themselves. The origami animals grew with the challenges and cheers, the games and tears. Their voices became stronger and more familiar. Friendships grew and were strengthened. They learned to trust each other and themselves. Time in the little playground showed them what love looks like.

Here and being reminded of what I desire and dream
Receiving this with confidence and as an affirmation
Expanding myself within a new commitment to release
what is already here

My desires and dreams had been planted within me
Growing and being nurtured all this time, until just
this right time
So instead of being ashamed, I am proud for all that is
happening now

For this moment and this progress has been awaiting for
just this time of awakening
This moment in time, is exactly where I am
supposed to be
To experience the fullness of transformation

Chapter 3
Try

Seasons passed, and OC grew a little older and stronger. Now she was able to play in the middle playground and enjoy the variety of challenges of an even higher platform to play the game of *Fly*. Still under the canopy of the cottonwoods, the middle playground was larger, with more challenging elements to play on and a place where animals could run, jump, climb, and slide. The animals grew in their strength and agility.

OC was more determined than ever to fly. She had new variations of the feelings of self-doubt and the excitement of getting closer to her dream of flying in the middle playground. Some friendships gave her the encouragement and the support she needed. Other friendships caused her to not feel good enough and made her doubt her dream.

And what did Owl really see? What did he really mean that I am made of a map? Did he mean a treasure map or something like the lines and colors that he has seen in the other animals? The giggles from her friends interrupted her thoughts, and her eyes scanned the new middle playground.

There were many ways OC had changed over the seasons in the park, many lessons learned in the previous playground, and now she was ready for something new. When she arrived at the middle playground, OC recognized Rabbit and Fox at play, and OC quickly tried to join in their games.

Rabbit and Fox had already made this new area their own, running and jumping through the new elements of play with ease. They were familiar with the middle playground and welcomed OC into this new place.

Unfolded

When OC first arrived, Rabbit asked Fox, "Do you think OC is ready to play here with us? She does not look old enough. Maybe she needs to stay where she was."

Fox replied, "OC is not like us, we are stronger and faster than she is. If she wants to play here, she will need to keep up. I doubt she is able. She is just a crane."

One day, OC was distracted while she was playing with her friends. She was mesmerized with the feathered birds flying around. Through the cottonwood trees, she noticed the glimmer of the sun on shiny airplanes gliding through the sky. The planes were flying so high beyond the canopy of the trees. At once, OC knew this was what she had been dreaming of the whole time. "An airplane!" OC exclaimed with her out loud voice.

Intuitive Rabbit hopped alongside OC and quickly remarked, "Don't be confused. You are a paper crane and not a feathered bird. You are a crane and are not a shiny plane. You should not dream of becoming a plane. You don't even know how to fly."

Try

OC thought for a moment, and more self-doubt began to rise. With her inside voice she said, "I have a dream of becoming a paper plane, but maybe Rabbit is right. Maybe I was meant to be a simple crane."

Owl sat on watch, and spoke to OC as if he heard the whisper inside her, "Be gentle when others speak to you with doubt and judgment. Listen to the voice inside you. Your strong inner voice reminds you of your beauty as a paper crane and the promise of your potential. Believe in yourself as you are and as you might become. Trust in small changes and the process of becoming more and more of who you are on the inside, your map. With kindness and love toward yourself, you will become free to fly."

> Be gentle when others speak to you with doubt and judgment. Listen to the voice inside you.

Slow moving Turtle once again overheard Owl speaking those words of wisdom to OC. He gradually walked over to OC and said, "Since I saw you behind the cottonwood trees 'checking on the roots' you have believed yourself to be more than an origami crane. Remember as young animals, we would practice flying off the swings and small platforms? Even then, I knew you were meant for more."

Unfolded

OC knew Turtle was right. She believed she was more, and yet did not know how to become the main character of her own dream.

So OC kept playing an older rendition of the game of *Fly* only with more strength and intensity. OC, Turtle, and YC would play *Fly* on the slide. OC's friends would line up at the bottom of the slide, creating more and more distance between them. As OC would slide down, she'd flap her wings harder and harder all the way until the end, where she would rise slightly in the air, catch a brief gust of wind, and float over Turtle and YC to land safely and sometimes unsafely on the ground.

Rabbit would join in, having created a special friendship with Turtle. He was ever encouraging and supportive of all the animals. Turtle was a friend to everyone and sensitive to their needs. He knew what it meant to be with other animals, to encourage them with joy and understanding. Rabbit liked herself more when she was around Turtle. She needed a friend who was slower to speak because her tendency to blurt out everything she was thinking and feeling often got her in trouble. Maybe Turtle could help her keep her foot out of her mouth.

Try

Over and again, OC's short flights and small crashes caused her to fall and second-guess herself. She realized she needed help to rise up again and fly. She learned that no matter what people say or how many times she falls to the ground, she had the strength needed within her to fulfill her dream. Maybe her dream was more than just a desire to fly. Maybe her longing went beyond being an origami crane.

OC continued to question everything. The older rendition of the game of *Fly* wasn't working. She kept trying harder, and nothing seemed to work out as she thought. OC wasn't sure if this game of *Fly* was something she should continue. She felt uncertain and tired of trying the same things over and over again and not succeeding. She was not getting any closer to her dream no matter how hard she tried. OC thought to herself, "Maybe Fox is right, I will never fly. Why should I try?"

Despite OC's fear and insecurity, she was unable to quiet her dream. The old ways weren't working. To fly, she needed to try something new.

Distracted again during all the games, OC asked herself, "What does new even look like?"

OC's friends knew when she was deep in thought. Just then her brother and closest friend, YC, interrupted her thoughts. "Do you really believe you have the ability to fly, OC? Because I think you can! How can I help?"

Turtle chimed in, "We know we can help you, but this may take some time. Where do we begin?"

OC was not sure how YC and Turtle could help, but she knew something significant needed to change. There was something about who she was that did not feel quite right. She felt at odds with her dream. How could she be both a paper crane and a paper plane? As OC watched the shiny planes in the sky, she noticed how the planes looked a bit different. Their shape was not the same as her shape. She noticed the planes had wings, but not like her wings.

OC closed her eyes remembering Owl's words. She was made of a map, but what did that mean? With the inspiration of a new form, she thought she might fly. OC's deep thoughts were interrupted by Turtle saying, "Let's go!"

"Coming," OC replied. Then she said, "Friends, maybe if I'm in another shape I may be able to reach my dream."

Rabbit laughed.

Try

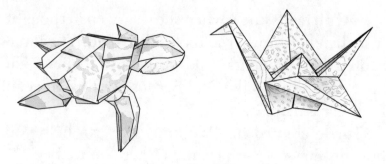

With her new inspiration, OC looked at YC and Turtle and said, "Can you help me add some folds to my wings? I know I have wings, but they aren't quite right. Let's try."

So YC and Turtle began to add some folds to one of OC's wings. It wasn't easy. OC's wings didn't want to have more folds. The wings were already tightly folded and creased. Adding some folds didn't seem possible. Discouragement grew not knowing what they were trying to do.

OC said, "Look up into the sky. See the airplanes soaring above the cottonwood trees? Do you see their shape? Do you see what their wings look like? Try that."

Her friends nodded.

Turtle offered, "I'm not sure we can add more folds. Maybe we need to unfold your wings to refold them."

"That's a great idea, Turtle." YC chimed in.

Turtle and YC began to unfold the tightly creased paper, but just one wing.

"Are you ok, OC? Does this hurt?" YC checked in.

"Yes, I am okay. The unfolding doesn't hurt; it's just uncomfortable." OC said.

> The unfolding doesn't hurt; it's just uncomfortable.

After some concerted effort and a little discomfort, YC and Turtle stared at the unfolded wing. "Sister, you are made of a map!" YC exclaimed to OC.

OC replied, "Great! I mean, what? A map? That is what Owl told me once. He said something about how my map will help me in some way, and I am not sure how yet."

Turtle added, "I overheard Owl share that with you. He said your map provides you with the clarity and confidence you need. You just need to look at your map and learn to read it. OC, look at your unfolded wing, *what do you see?*"

OC paused and chuckled because slow-moving Turtle often found himself overhearing something or another. He was such a good friend to her. He used his patience, listening skills, and slow pace to bear witness and speak truth when the timing was right.

OC smiled at Turtle and then looked closely at her newly unfolded paper wing. She had never noticed this part of her before. Part of her map kind of looked like Owl's paper. She interrupted her own

33

Try

thoughts distracting her and instructed her friends: "Now fold that wing so it looks like the plane's wing." OC said.

And they began refolding one of OC's paper wings that gave her time to return to her own thoughts. "Did YC say I was made of a map? That's what Owl told me. And Turtle heard it, too. This must be more important than I can understand right now."

Turtle and YC unfolded and refolded her wing into a new shape like a plane and the other wing was still in the form of a crane. Rabbit had joined in on the wing project, but in the middle of the process Rabbit couldn't help herself but say to OC, "Are you sure we should do this? Maybe this isn't the right thing to do."

"Keep going. I want to fly." OC said to her friends.

Nearby, Fox thought everyone was wasting their time. Fox ran in a circle around them and laughed at OC, "You look so ridiculous. You will never fly. Why try?"

"Keep going," OC said to Turtle, YC, and Rabbit. OC fought back her tears.

As the three friends continued to work together to make this transformation a reality, OC's anticipation increased. "There," Turtle said, announcing the completion of a plane wing.

Owl observed the unfolding process and knew something special was happening. With a sense of pride and joy, Owl kept a curious watch over the animals.

With one wing reformed, OC thought, "Now I believe I can fly, so let's try!" OC began to make her way to the middle platform. She believed even more that her new shape and the higher platform was what she needed to fly.

The friends and even Fox went to the edge of the platform, anxious with anticipation.

YC encouraged OC, "You now have a new plane wing to fly!"

Turtle said, "You have the courage. Why not try?" So OC did. She leapt off the middle platform. Her left crane wing flapped like usual. Her new right plane wing stayed steady.

You have the courage. Why not try?

The friends covered their eyes as OC took a hard right spiral off the platform.

When OC's friends opened their eyes, they saw the furry Golden tending to OC. Sometimes a puppy is just what is needed. Golden panted and nudged OC back to standing with his nose. He was a retriever after all.

This attempt to fly was not what OC expected. Her doubt and anxiety grew. She just wanted to see if she could fly with her newly folded wing. OC then had a new idea as she was comforted by Golden.

OC asked Golden, the playful puppy, to help. OC jumped onto the puppy's back, held on tight, and commanded, "Run!" Golden immediately began to run as fast as he could. Together they tore through the playground, Golden's tail wagging with a big smile on his face.

OC's friends stared in amazement, eyes wide open this time.

"Maybe this wasn't a great idea," Turtle said.

But YC kept cheering.

Rabbit remarked, "Riding on Golden's back is not flying. That doesn't count."

As Golden ran around the perimeter of the playground, OC held onto his fur, her eyes getting bigger and bigger as she felt a surge of energy and excitement. OC flapped her left crane wing with all of her strength, her right plane wing firmly pressed in place. OC knew it was almost time. She lowered her head in determination.

As OC and the puppy approached the cotton-wood trees. She yelled, "Golden, STOP!"

And so obediently, he stopped.

With that sudden action, OC was launched off Golden's back and shot straight forward and up into the air, her left wing flapping as hard as it could, and the reformed right plane wing held steady in place. With all her effort, OC began to rise upward, circling to the right, rising higher, with the short flight ending as she flew directly into the trunk of one of the two cottonwood trees.

OC tumbled to the ground.

"Good dog," Fox laughed.

OC landed awkwardly on the ground. She felt a new discomfort in her wings. And she was a bit dizzy from flying in circles.

The first moments of this flight were exhilarating, and the next few moments were scary. OC looked at herself and noticed why she felt a bit of pain: one of her wings was crumpled and the other was bent. Her tail looked broken, and another part of her body was a bit crinkled. Feeling hurt, ashamed for trying, and embarrassed with her effort, she hadn't succeeded. She didn't know what hurt worse, the physical or the emotional pain.

While OC was sitting on the ground bruised and bent, Fox ran toward her with a certain look in his eyes. He was yelping as he ran, circling

Try

OC as she sat in the dirt. He kept mocking OC singing, "You cannot fly! Why try? You cannot fly! Why try?"

Fox continued to circle OC as she sat alone. He said, "I told you. You will never fly. Why try? You belong in the playground, not up in the sky. That is where the feathered birds belong, not you."

Rabbit was next to arrive, "See, I told you it was a bad idea to change your wings. Birds can fly, not you. You should accept who you are, a crane. What did you expect was going to happen? Getting hurt should remind you that you are not good enough to fly high."

YC's gleeful voice drowned out the rest, shouting "You did it. You did it!"

A little later, Turtle arrived and said, "You are so brave, OC."

"When is the next flight, OC?" Asked YC.

Rabbit remarked, "The next flight? You should not try again unless you want to get hurt again."

Turtle had enough of Rabbit and said, "I have been hurt in the past, too. With my shell, people think I do not feel the same things others feel, but I do. When I am hurt, it is more difficult for others to notice. My healing happens on the inside

> Healing begins by accepting ourselves just as we are.

first. Healing begins by accepting ourselves just as we are. Let's give OC some space."

Fox said, "Yes, give her some space. Come on, everybody. I'll race you to the slide. Maybe OC stands for Origami Crash."

OC hung her head.

Owl swooped in as the rest of the animals headed for the slide.

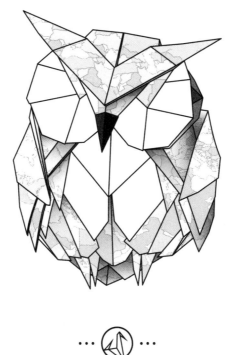

··· ⟨🐦⟩ ···

Owl was watching this whole event from his perch in the playground. He comforted OC with his presence.

Up close, Owl noticed the crumples, bends and folds, the new wing, and the disappointment in OC's eyes. He asked, "How was the flight?"

OC responded, "I don't know. Good, I guess. I think I was onto something with the new wing, and of course Golden helped. I got dizzy flying in circles and was scared. Now, look at me. I'm a failure. I'm embarrassed from hitting the tree and falling to the ground."

Owl prompted, "Tell me more about your new wing."

OC thought a bit, and said, "It did not feel like I thought it would. The folding, unfolding, and refolding happened so fast. I noticed new parts of my paper just beneath some of the old folds. I guess it kind of looked like a map. That's what you told me, right? Anyway, next thing I know I'm on Golden's back."

Owl prompted again, "Tell me more about your new wing."

"My wing? The new folds kind of worked. Wait, are you saying I should try the other wing too? Was I just unbalanced? You're right. I will try again."

OC brushed herself off and was about to meet her friends at the slide when Owl reminded her, "Remember the answers are already within you when you learn how to read your map. You are made from a map; your very nature is here to help you on your journey to fly. Trust the map. Trust the process. When it comes to understanding the truth of who you are, and how to fulfill your dream, there is no better map to lead the way than the map inside of you. Maps show the way. Maps have clues to where you've been, how you've grown, and all the memories and emotions in between."

> There is no better map to lead the way than the map inside of you.

OC nodded. Now she was more confused about what Owl was talking about.

Owl went back to his perch in the playground. He looked down at OC and said, "There is a light beyond the shadow of the branches, you will get there and be warmed by the sun above. Continue to try and fly, guided by the light within you, *your light will find the light, your light will give you flight.*"

41

Try

The miracle of our unfolding is a declaration of our
possibility
An act of freedom, curiosity, and hope
Discovering our indisputable and intentional beauty

The promise of this process lies in our becoming
In the releasing of the tremendous gift of life
That is already living within you
An unlimited expression of self
The fulfilling of your dream
For you and all humanity

This potential is here, closer than you know
It's only one unfolding away

Chapter 4
Fly

A new season in the playground began the day of that first real flight.

"Who's ready for my next flight?" OC asked her friends. She was a bit crumpled.

Without saying a word, the origami friends answered her question as they walked together in unison from the slide to the third section of the playground for the oldest of origami animals. Here, there were taller rope ladders, longer slides, monkey bars, a climbing wall, and higher platforms than anywhere else on the playground. Here was play that took all kinds of strength and imagination. In this playground, the play moved fast. The origami animals couldn't help but be more confident in their activities.

This part of the playground was not directly beneath the cottonwoods, and there was a clearer view of the sky above the playground. There was also a gateway in this part of the park leading to a path yet to be explored. More than any other section of the playground, this was where trust was tested and more risks were taken. Through conflict and change, each origami animal learned more about who they are, their beliefs, and their relationships.

The slow walk to the big part of the playground was silent. Even Rabbit kept her mouth shut. Even Turtle thought the walk was taking forever. Fox bit his tongue; even he knew it would cross a line to make fun of Origami Crash out loud.

YC broke the silence with his joy. "Now what, OC?"

All the origami animals looked at OC and realized how crumpled, bent, and deformed OC was. She was at the same time stronger, wiser, and had more resolve.

"I need help to fly. I think we were onto something with the new folds. Other than the crashes, the one refolded wing was really working," OC explained.

"If you mean causing you to spin like a tornado, then I know what you mean," said Rabbit.

All the animals giggled, even OC.

Fox, not able to help himself said, "OC, why not whirl?"

The laughter continued and OC replied, "Exactly! If I can whirl, why can't I fly?"

Fox shook his head. His punch didn't land like he wanted.

OC always knew she was different from the rest of the animals. As she grew, this realization became more and more clear. OC felt there was nothing wrong with being an origami crane, but something inside of OC needed to be discovered and set free. This transformation would need a little more planning than just winging it. The dream of flight was within reach.

"Let us know when you're ready," said Turtle. The animals left OC and hung out by the monkey bars and ropes.

OC closed her eyes and began to imagine herself flying, soaring high above the cottonwood trees, above the playground, and into the great blue sky above. She even pictured some of the other animals going through a similar transformation. She knew she was ready to fly high.

OC knew a little self-talk wouldn't hurt. "I have what it takes to fly. I believe in myself. I can create the life that I dream of to release the identity within me without any shame or guilt, criticism, or judgment. I can fly."

> I have what it takes to fly. I believe in myself. I can create the life that I dream of.

Owl from above slowly blinked his eyes in delight. He overheard her positive affirmations.

He called down to OC, "What do you see?"

OC answered, "I see myself flying, but I can't fly in the shape I'm in."

Owl answered, "In your unfolding and refolding, your friends and you found a new shape. You are still OC. There is nothing about *you* that needs to change. Others will help you. If you want to fly, you need to try."

OC found her friends and admitted that she needed help. "Who can help me unfold and refold my wings?" Her friends rallied around her. Even Fox.

In the midst of the folding and unfolding, OC distracted herself with daydreams "Look at those shiny planes soaring above the branches of the cottonwood trees. I really want to fly like those planes." Turns out it was her out-loud voice.

Fox laughed and said, "We can fold you some better wings, but you will never fly. Why try? You will never be like the planes. You do not have the strength nor confidence to fly like that."

Everyone stopped. "Maybe we should take a break," Turtle advised. The friends headed over to the slide and gave OC a chance to regroup.

While taking turns going down the smooth polished slide, Turtle began to think of new ideas and plans.

Unfolded

Turtle asked, "What if both of her wings were in the shape of a plane's wings? Maybe we should help unfold and refold the other side. Could we try that?"

YC summoned OC to the bottom of the slide. "Sister, we have a great idea! Turtle, tell her."

OC met them at the slide and listened to Turtle's idea. Filled with hope again, she responded, "Let's try."

So they did.

It soon became clear that to make the best paper plane, OC needed to be completely unfolded. The friends worked together to continue OC's unfolding from a beautiful paper crane. Her creases and the crumpled parts were now sort of smoothed out. As the process continued, OC began to feel more like she could really fly. Her excitement grew.

Half-heartedly, Rabbit was helping with Turtle's idea. When all of a sudden she caught her reflection in the shiny slide. Fear gripped her by the ears. For the first time in her life, she was at a loss for words by what she saw, a reflection of a map. Rabbit glanced back and forth between the mirrored slide and OC. Rabbit wondered if it was really true that she too was made of a map. She was terrified of what that might mean.

47

Fly

To interrupt her own inner discomfort, Rabbit turned back to OC and her friends. Rabbit saw that OC was now a flat paper square map and she shouted, "Oh no! Look what you've done. You shouldn't be doing that! What if you could never go back to a crane?"

Fox laughed, "Squares don't fly."

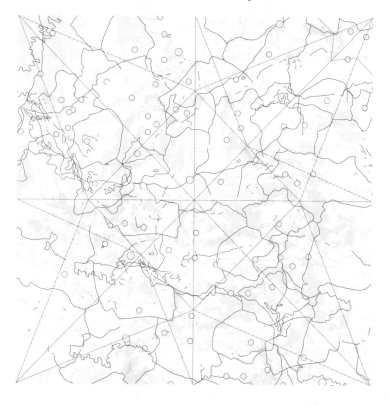

Fox and Rabbit left to climb on the rope ladders. OC had not thought about never going back to her old self. She was YC's sister and a good friend to the other animals. Would she never be a crane again? Would anyone recognize her?

"Wait. What? I'm a square?" OC began to doubt herself and looked to Turtle for help.

Turtle said, "We have a plan and a process, and I believe we can fold you back into a sleek crane if you want to."

YC assured his big sister, "You're not just a square. You are a map!"

OC asked YC, "What do you see, YC?"

YC answered, "I see thick blue circles, brown thin lines, green shapes, and a bunch of words."

OC thanked YC and said, "Remember what you saw, YC. And remind me later. It's time to fold."

Turtle and YC used some of the original creases to create a form with different wings. They smoothed out the old wrinkles and spent the needed time to work out each new design detail until the origami crane finally became a paper plane.

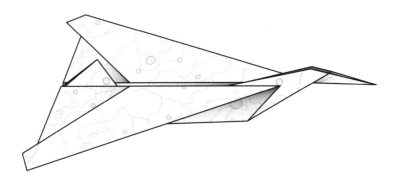

"That's different." Rabbit remarked coming back from the ropes.

Now in a new form, it was time for OC to test her dream. She needed to trust in herself more than ever and trust in her friends to help her fly. She made her way up to the highest platform in the big playground, determined to attempt her dream to fly.

Rabbit and Fox were waiting at the top, they were already jumping off the edge as they always have done. But when OC glanced over the edge of the platform, she realized she was much higher than she thought. She was nervous.

She made several attempts to leap off the highest platform only to skid to a stop just before the edge, shaking in fear. Fox and Rabbit were there on the platform trying to discourage OC from flying because they could sense something was different now.

During one attempt, Rabbit stood in front of OC and said, "You might be a paper plane now, but with all those creases, you probably won't be able to fly. Why do you keep trying? You have never done this before, and you're probably going to fall right to the ground."

She did fall to the ground on the first leap off the big platform.

During another attempt, Fox ran in front of OC and knocked her off balance, causing one of her wings to bend. Fox smirked at OC and said, "You will never fly. Why try?"

OC didn't know if Fox's words or actions hurt more.

She fell again.

OC did not expect this type of resistance from two of her friends. Owl, watching from a nearby branch, asked OC, "How are you feeling? Are their messages about you true?"

OC was feeling the familiar self-doubt and fear rise within her again, and wondered if her dream to fly would ever happen. She replied to Owl, "They have always told me this. Maybe what they are saying is true."

Fly

Owl asked, "Is their message about you actually true?"

OC paused and replied, "It feels true. Now, I'm just a paper plane that can't fly."

Owl looked OC in the eyes and reminded her, "There will always be people who do not believe in you. Whenever you hear their voices, remind yourself of your inner strength. If you want to fly, you need to try."

> There will always be people who do not believe in you. Whenever you hear their voices, remind yourself of your inner strength. If you want to fly, you need to try.

With a greater sense of determination, she tried again. Moving to the back of the platform, she took a deep breath and composed herself.

Remembering Owl's question, "What do you see?" She whispered to herself, "I see myself in flight."

With clarity and renewed confidence at the back of the platform, OC took several more deep breaths. Now relaxed and ready, she began to run toward

Unfolded

the edge. Gaining speed and excitement, her confidence began to increase and the anticipation of what was about to happen caused OC's eyes and smile to widen.

Once OC left the platform, she was quickly lifted by the breezes, up and upward, navigating through the branches of the cottonwood trees and briefly flying with the feathered birds and circling the trees. Giddy with glee, she was soaring in the blue skies above where the great planes were soaring effortlessly through the clouds.

OC felt different sensations and thoughts in this new environment of the sky. She felt as if she was rising above the shadows of doubt, fear, and disbelief. She rose through the shadows of the branches, navigating through the canopy of complexity the branches provided. Effortlessly rising even higher, she caught a view of the vast world beyond the park. Until finally she soared upon the winds of self-acceptance and freedom.

As she flew into the sky, OC realized she had really become something new, a paper plane. In flight, she felt a thrill she had never experienced before. As she flew higher and higher, the wind rushed past her wings. The freedom of flight filled her being. She laughed with joy and marveled at the world from a whole new perspective.

As she flew, OC began to feel something unfamiliar. Living your dream shouldn't result in a sense of unease. In the moment, she missed the intricate folds and delicate details of her origami crane form. She wondered if she had made a mistake in dreaming, transforming, and now flying. She did not want to forget where she came from. She did not want to give up her new ability to fly.

In that tension, she soared over the park, above the two great cottonwood trees. She spotted her friends watching from the playground below. The origami animals were laughing, playing together, and trying to make new games of their own. She felt a sense of nostalgia and longing as she watched them at play.

OC shouted to her friends from the skies above, "I am flying! I am free! I am me!"

YC glanced up and said to Turtle, "I always believed her dream would come true."

Turtle agreed. "To fly is what is right about OC. To fly is her dream becoming a reality. I also dream and try, and my dream looks different from her dream. I may be slow to move and slow to change, but I will always make progress. Believe in your process, celebrate your progress, and you will one day fly higher than you ever dreamed."

From the playground, YC continued to watch his sister with great excitement, and shouted toward her, "I love you, OC! Keep going! Keep flying, you are almost there!"

Believe in your process, celebrate your progress, and you will one day fly higher than you ever dreamed.

OC flew higher and higher. OC felt the cooling breezes of the skies and felt the warmth of the sun on her little paper wings. OC continued to soar and began to trust her new ability even more, realizing she knew how to fly the whole time. OC was free. She belonged among the shiny planes. This might be home, she thought.

Glancing down one last time, OC saw the playground below, her friends watching her fly further and further away. OC noticed the neighborhood surrounding the playground, the lakes and ponds glistening in the sunlight, and the great landscapes stretching out toward the horizon.

Then, OC began to feel a strong presence drawing near and became nervous. Looking side to side, she saw a great bird in flight making its way towards her. She had never seen such a flier like that before.

A mighty eagle was now flying alongside OC with great confidence and ease. Eagle said to OC, "Welcome to the blue sky, I'm Eagle. I have not seen you here before. Are you new to flying?"

OC felt proud to be recognized, and replied, "Yes, I'm OC. I am new to flying. I always knew that I was meant to fly and getting here has not been easy."

Eagle gestured to OC to follow, as she flew through the sky.

Eagle asked, "Is flying what you thought it would be?"

OC replied, "It is even more than I could imagine. I never knew there was so much to discover. I thought our playground was so big and challenging. Now, I see a world much bigger than I had ever imagined."

Eagle heard OC's excitement and curiosity. When Eagle was young, she, too, learned to fly and gain confidence, exploring more with each flight. Eagle knew OC needed some encouragement in this new experience of flying and all the sensations she might be feeling.

Eagle and OC continued to fly together, taking in all the new sights and sounds of flight. They watched the shiny planes overhead effortlessly gliding by. Eagle pointed out several unique characteristics of the landscape below; the green grasses of the fields, the glistening of the water that looked like blue circles. The moving cars along thin brown roads, the city, the neighborhoods, and even other playgrounds where origami animals played together.

OC thought for a moment and said, "I feel so alive and free! I never imagined a world so big and different. Flying is easier than I thought it would be. But when I return to my friends in the playground, what will they think about how much I have changed?"

Eagle smiled and responded, "Have you really changed all that much? You said you were meant to fly. Your friends have probably known this about you, too. They may not be that surprised at all."

> Have you really changed all that much? You said you were meant to fly. Your friends have probably known this about you, too. They may not be that surprised at all.

Together, OC and Eagle continued to soar through the sky above the playgrounds, roads, and water below. After a little while longer, OC turned to Eagle and said, "Thank you for flying with me and encouraging me to fly even higher. I have to go back now."

Eagle nodded and looked OC in the eye and spoke with clarity and compassion, "You have been transformed. You tested yourself by risking to fly. Accept your imperfections. Be at peace with the folds and the creases from before. Learn lessons and apply your wisdom. When you return to the playground, be kind and share."

OC thanked Eagle, and began her return to the playground. She learned that reaching her dreams was something to be held and cherished. Her dream was to be shared and taught to others.

All things have intention
A purpose to every fold
For me to release my potential
I need to ease my anxious hold

My journey has brought me far
My doubt was faced, my form was changed
Lessons were learned, relationships grown
I gained a new courage
I came into my own

I have leaned into doubt with courage
I have moved past the edges of fear
I have moved from the shadows into light
I have new wings, I am now in flight

Fly

Chapter 5
Home

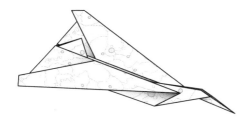

OC returned to the park in a soft landing between the branches of the cottonwood trees. Excitement filled her whole being as did exhaustion. Newly formed as a plane, and still recognizable as OC, the curious origami animals watched from the monkey bars. She was home.

Owl was the first to meet OC.

Owl asked, "How did it go?"

OC started rambling on about what she saw, how she felt, and who she met.

Owl listened and offered, "Remember, to learn to fly is to learn to love. To love and accept yourself for who you are. To love yourself in the shadows beneath the trees. To love yourself in the light of the clear blue skies. To love yourself with those who doubt and criticize you. And to love yourself among those who love you most. Keep flying, and don't forget to land and love."

> Remember, to learn to fly is to learn to love. To love and accept yourself for who you are.

Owl went back to his perch as the friends circled OC.

"I knew you could do it!" YC exclaimed, flapping his wings trying to leave the ground, too.

Rabbit was skeptical, and Fox was cynical. They wore their sense of disbelief as they faced the joy on OC's face.

Fox spoke first, "You really did not fly as well as you think you did. And if you try again, I am sure you will not fly. You got lucky."

Rabbit added, "You should never have done that. Origami cranes are not meant to fly. And now YC thinks he can fly too."

"Well, maybe I can," YC said.

OC couldn't tell what Turtle was thinking. He was quiet.

OC's joy and fulfillment were quickly replaced by doubt and fear. Her inner dialogue mirrored the questioning of her friends. "What if I try again? Will I fail? What if I was not meant to fly after all? Why couldn't I be happy just being a crane?"

Owl from above, came down to address OC in front of the origami animals. Owl knew that she was meant to fly all along. He knew her life was changed by this experience. OC's change would affect everybody.

So Owl spoke with a gentle voice, for all to hear, "OC, you have changed. You have lived your dream. With help from your friends you became a paper plane. You flew higher than you ever imagined. You were set free. And sometimes our dreams affect our friends."

> With help from your friends you became a paper plane. You flew higher than you ever imagined. You were set free.

YC cheered, "Like me! You inspired me to find my dream."

Rabbit turned to YC and said, "No, OC ruined you. You should be happy with who you are."

YC hung his head.

Fox piled on and said, "OC, you should never do that again. You are an origami crane, not a paper plane. You are supposed to remain in the park. I'm sure Turtle will help fold you back into a paper crane. Right, Turtle?"

Turtle was still silent.

Fox laughed, interpreting Turtle's silence as agreement to not help OC. Fox continued. "Looks like you're stuck like that, OC. Turns out your dream ruined you, too. You will never fly again. Why try?" Rabbit added, "Is it really worth all of this discomfort? Are you sure this dream is right for you? If this dream was meant to be, it would come easier to you."

Fox said, "Just accept what you are. You are an origami crane, not a paper plane. You are trying to change something that is not meant to change, that is why it hurts so much. This is your own fault."

OC heard her friends talking, but for some reason, she couldn't really hear them. Her mind was still in the skies above.

YC had sided up to Turtle who was yet to speak. YC quietly asked Turtle, "Do you think it is too late for me to fly? Can I still try?"

Turtle slowly turned his head and looked YC in the eyes. YC noticed Turtle's tears. Turtle said tenderly, "It's never too late to live your dream, YC. Is flying your dream?"

64

Unfolded

YC nodded his head in agreement. He didn't know if flying was his dream, but he wanted to have a dream just like OC, too.

"Stop whispering, jokers," Fox shouted.

Rabbit laughed.

"Enough!" OC answered.

And then OC smiled. "Having a dream is one thing. Living that dream is another. I couldn't have lived my dream without you all. Even you, Fox. YC, I want you to find your dream, and we'll help you live it. And Turtle, why the tears?"

Turtle finally spoke with an extra slow voice, "Well, I was happy playing *Fly* when we were little. I guess I never really wanted to fly, but I sure had fun helping you find your new form to help you fly. We can help you fold back to a crane, another shape, or whatever you want. I guess I'm proud of you. I kind of want to know what you saw in the sky."

OC took the opening, "Aww, thanks for asking, Turtle. I saw all kinds of things. You can see so much more from up there. I met a new friend, Eagle, and she helped me, too. From up in the sky I could see the green grasses of the fields, the glistening of the water that looked like thick blue circles. I could even see cars moving along thin brown roads. I saw the horizon, the clouds, the city, the neighborhoods, and even other playgrounds where other origami animals played together."

65

Home

YC exclaimed in his youthful jubilance, "OC! The map! You saw your map. You told me to remember green areas, thick blue circles, thin brown lines, and words."

Everyone went quiet. Turtle cried again.

OC broke the silence. "Yes, YC. Wow. Great memory. I am made of a map. All I ever needed was inside me. Turtle, what is happening now?"

Turtle said, "We all are made of maps. Our dreams and answers are within us. If we have a dream, why not try?"

YC announced. "If I'm a map, I want to fly like OC, too. Who will help me?" Everyone agreed to help. Even Fox.

Unfolded

OC began to reflect on all the lessons Owl taught her over the years. She remembered all that she had learned and experienced by flying with Eagle. She knew she could help her little brother, YC, learn to fly, but it would be his story. If he wanted to, he could learn to fly high above the cottonwoods just like his sister. YC was excited to learn, having played the game of *Fly* through all the years. He had his own feelings of self-doubt, and questioned what it might take to fly. If OC could fly, so could he. YC had watched his older sister learn to risk and face challenges. His transformation into a little map paper plane was different and a bit quicker.

All the origami friends helped in the first few steps of unfolding YC. The friends showed more patience with a plan this time around. Then Fox went looking for the puppy, Golden, to help another crane crash.

Once unfolded fully into a square, YC asked, "Am I a map, too?"

OC answered, "Why, yes, you are. We will get you refolded and you can start practicing your flight. Be patient, dear brother. Our potential is released through patience and practice."

OC reflected while YC practiced with Golden's help. "There are lessons in life that can only be learned through taking flight. To fly, we must accept and face our self-doubt and fear coming from our memories of past experiences and failed attempts at flight. To fly is to face our dream with courage and the longing to be free."

> There are lessons in life that can only be learned through taking flight.

> To fly is to face our dream with courage and the longing to be free.

Folded anew, YC went to the top platform with his sister, OC. He went to the back, ready for a running start. He took deep breaths like his sister did and imagined himself in flight. YC shouted to OC, "Do you think this is possible?"

OC answered with a smile and a nod, "In a world of possibilities, why not fly?"

My dream is now a light
A light that flows through me

I surrender doubt and criticism
I welcome this new truth within
A truth about myself
Others, and a place in this world
I set myself free
Free to be me

So now I trust anew
In this moment and in the place
I believe in who I am
And trust in my discoveries

To be wholly as we are
Just as we are
Knowing all is well

With our heart as a guide
With hope, we inspire and try
We no longer act in fear
Now, we fly

Home

Reflection and Application

Stories give us a way to connect as humans. Stories infuse meaning into our ordinary existence. There are universal threads in human stories. A good story can ignite action and make the complex simple to understand. We are each living our own story. Listening to one another's stories is sacred work.

The hope is to inspire a curiosity compassion, and courage to live our life's story to its fullest. Life is a really good teacher and so are our dreams.

The Reflection and Application sections that follow offer handles and prompts for reflection.

What Stands Out?

It is important to name thoughts and emotions that capture our attention or ignite our imagination, and then go a step further: to reflect intentionally so we can act meaningfully and relationally. One's identity is where to start when trying to understand how dreams can unlock our greatest potential.

There are many ways to understand our unique talents and abilities, and most people use assessment tools, coaching, and mindfulness practices to reach a better understanding of who we are on the inside. In *Unfolded*, OC discovers her unique identity through her pursuit of the dream to fly. And it is in this journey she begins to realize two things: her current shape needs to change, and she is made of a map. Whatever OC needed to reach her goals has been within her all along.

In this Reflection and Application section, linger with the parts that get you curious. There is no formal order or progression. So, you can create your own. Spoiler alert: depending on the area of your life, you could see yourself in many of this book's chapters.

Shaping People and Places

"Describe a person who or place that has shaped who you are." This simple prompt gives us a moment of pause to remember the shaping influences that have folded and molded us into the people we are today.

To describe a shaping person or place gives an indicator of one's perspective, what we care about, and why specific defining moments have been key to our growth. Many of the characters in the story represent the amalgamation of people we meet throughout our lives. The playgrounds are developmental or challenging places of growth in our stories. Our identity is profoundly shaped by the people and places of our lives; they provide the unique textures and outlines, folds and creases of our map that we carry to this day.

The Characters

Many people help us in pursuing our dreams and unfolding our greatest potential. Are there people in our lives representing each of the characters? Which of the following "voices" do we represent to others? And which "voice" is most like our inner voice?

> OC (Origami Crane): represents anyone who has ever had a dream. OC is not afraid to dream, even though she struggles with self-doubt and fear. She is confident in her dream, willing to ask for help and learn, not afraid to try, and relies on her friends to help her reach her potential. Most importantly, she helps others with their dreams, too.
> YC (Young Crane): represents joy, optimism, and happiness. YC is the smallest of all the animals and brings a youthful enthusiasm to the friends

in the playground. He loves his sister, OC, and this bond gives him the inspiration to believe in his own dreams.

Owl: represents wisdom and insight. The oldest of all the animals, Owl is a wise sage and mentor who is guiding OC and all the other animals along their journey of dreaming, self-discovery, healing, and believing in oneself. From his perch, he is always on watch.

Turtle: represents the perspective of development and growth. He is gentle, steady, and patient. His voice reflects the lessons he learns from his experience and also his keen observations of others. Of all the animals he remained curious and kind to his friends. He was around at just the right time.

Rabbit: represents shame and guilt. Rabbit is always on alert, ready to move quickly, and is cautious of danger. Her use of shame and guilt are a way to defend and protect herself, and she means no harm to the other animals really.

Fox: represents criticism and judgment. Fox is older and thinks he's more mature than the rest of the animals, except Owl. He is always around, though we may not see him. Fox is quick to criticize and judge because of his own deep insecurities.

Reflection and Application

Golden: represents loyalty and companionship. Golden is a golden retriever puppy and a playful companion to all the animals. He is full of life and is willing to be there for whatever you need. Be careful what you ask for because Golden is blindly obedient.

Eagle: represents courage, confidence, and experience. Eagle represents that person in our lives who has lived and risked, has gained experience through a variety of challenges, and has the confidence to show for it. Quick to recognize and name potential, Eagle is there to encourage you to believe even more in yourself and fly higher.

To name the voices around us helps give insight to our self-talk, our team dynamics, or family drama. Think about the voices of optimism and positivity, encouragement and support, guilt and shame, criticism and judgment, wisdom and guidance, and mature influence. All voices have a shaping impact on our identity and dreams.

The Playground

Playgrounds represent the places and experiences that have shaped who we are as individuals. A playground may provide different opportunities of growth teaching us coordination, skills, taking risks, and building strength. The playgrounds of our lives could be where we attended school, a neighborhood, community, a job or profession, or a season of life. Playgrounds change over time and are gathering places designed for play, experimentation, practice, and trust.

Where is your playground? What types of challenges and opportunities do you face there? Who is in the playground with you? And what do they represent to you?

We cannot change some of the playgrounds of our life and the people within them. We can choose the playgrounds and some of the people in the future to help us unfold our greatest potential in pursuit of our dreams. In each scenario, we learn to integrate, adapt, and live with all of it. Remember, the playgrounds have a shaping influence on reaching our dreams and releasing our potential.

Map

We are each made of a map: an internal landscape that is uniquely our own. A landscape holds all the talent and strength, courage and confidence, compassion and empathy, lessons and wisdom we will ever need to pursue our greatest dreams.

Reflection and Application

Our map is shaped by how we were parented, by whom and when. Our map points to key relationships, lived experiences, culture of origin, surrounding environment, lessons learned, and wisdom gained.

Each of these factors, along with our biology and genetics, have created the deep valley folds, the high mountain folds, and all the creases and bends that have given us the shape we are in today. *And the shape you are today, is not the shape you need to stay.*

The value of dreaming lies in discovering the unique topography and design of our map. This discovery happens within the process of unfolding and refolding. We all have the ability to reshape the expression of who we are, unlocking our potential and unleashing our creativity. Unfolding and reshaping helps us to overcome our fears and step into their truest selves, achieving a sense of joy and fulfillment in both our personal and professional lives.

From Dream to Home: Which chapter stood out to you?

DREAM: Name It

Why are dreams important? Dreams play a key role in helping fulfill our greatest potential. A dream does not have to be our own dream. A dream can be inspired by a compelling vision, a humanitarian cause, a family value, a relationship, or a career goal. Whatever the form, a dream can significantly impact our life.

At times we need to be invited to dream, to reimagine a dream, or to let a dream go. Sometimes it's time to dream a new dream, to inspire others to dream, or to help someone else make their dream a reality. When dreams unfold, clues about your identity and greatest potential lie in the creases.

Is there a dream you are pursuing now? Are you grateful for a dream that did not come true? Have you ever realized you were living someone else's dream for your life?

Like OC, for her to fulfill her dream she needed to change. The shape she began with was not the shape she needed to stay. To accept an invitation to dream is a step to unfold the greatest potential within you. Our greatest and most exciting potential might be just one unfolding away.

When the dream is about to launch, notice what is needed to unlearn. Note where you need to be unfolded to be folded anew. In the moment of being unfolded, we may feel the absence of a recognizable form.

Owl asked, "What do you see?"

Reflection and Application

PLAY: Practice in Disguise

As kids, we often have a chance to play at school, play firefighter, or play explorer. Play itself has changed a lot in our lifetimes. It was not long ago that play happened exclusively without parent or adult supervision. Children were allowed to get to a playground themselves, figure out what games to play, how to get along with others, problem-solve, and settle disputes usually without an adult in sight. Things have changed. Playgrounds now come with warning signs.

Whatever play looks like, it will involve your imagination, willingness to work with others, and an expectation that our skills will be tested. Pay attention to what types of play brings you joy and joy to others.

Think of the early experiences when you enjoyed playing. Imagine the games that helped you grow, enjoy the practice, and invite others to play together. Who was there with you? And what did you learn?

No matter what stage of the story OC found herself, she and her friends were always playing together. Play reinforces how intentional practice builds our skills, teases our capacities, and invites us to make changes. When we play, we learn how to get along with others, how to take turns, and how to be innovative and creative within our play. Our playgrounds often change as we grow.

Owl replied warmly, "For your dream to grow, you will need to let go. You will experience failure, and you will experience success. Each time you try, you will learn, adapt, and try again. If you stay in this play-ground too long, your dream will be limited by what becomes familiar."

TRY: Practice with Intention

Multiple tries will teach you a lot. A dream can invite us over and again to keep trying. In this pro-cess, we will face self-doubt and fear and be given the chance to accept the changes made.

Believe in yourself. Be ready for the voices that amplify your inner thoughts and creativity. Those comments might hurt more than the pain of flying into your proverbial branches, hitting the trunk of the cottonwood, and falling to the ground. Some friends will have different perspectives than you. They might not believe in your potential, or might be afraid of their own potential. Keep trying and practicing. There is still more to come.

When have you needed to try something new to achieve a dream? Was this difficult to practice? What lessons in this season of try do you still prac-tice today?

When we try, we learn we need help. We may need help in our process of unfolding and refolding. We also have great potential to unfold and refold ourselves. As we try, this process of unfolding and noticing, dreaming and refolding, will lead us to discover our greatest potential for change and growth.

In our unfolded state we represent our potential to become the person we are created to be. Here, with the lines and creases of our lives ever present, we let go of the form they represent to use some original folds in the refolding process. And as we pay attention to our full identity, this too is the patient process of becoming.

Owl said, "There is a light beyond the shadow of the branches, you will get there and be warmed by the sun above. Continue to try and fly, guided by the light within you, your light will find the light, your light will give you flight."

FLY: Go for It

The exhilaration of a launch, the awareness of meeting a need and tasting the sweetness of a dream. There is nothing quite like it. What is it for you? Have there been moments in your life when you had the opportunity to humbly savor the achievement of your dream?

In a world of possibilities, why not fly? The metaphor of fly illustrates the feeling we experience when we fulfill our dream. Fly can also illustrate the feeling of accomplishment at any stage in the process of pursuing a dream, whether we reach it or not. To "fly" is to ask for help, to start unfolding, refolding, to practice, and to test ourselves. Remember, to "fly" is our connection with the power of a dream to unfold our greatest potential.

Who has been inspirational to you flying? What was it like to be in flight? How did you feel? Was flying all it's cracked up to be?

Our greatest potential and power for flight lies in our willingness to embrace the process and receiving help from others in whatever form this help arrives. Our confidence lies in the assurance that all we need is here, within us.

OC, remembering Owl's question, "What do you see?" whispered to herself, "I see myself in flight."

HOME: Reflect and Share

Home can be a place of rest, an intentional pause for purposeful reflection, or an opportunity to help others reach for their dream. Home gives us a new playground to share with others what we've learned. Home let's us take a breath to try again, dream further, or practice something new. Home just might be the place where a new dream is birthed.

For the first time or once again, the moment we realize our life's journey has brought us to the place where we are faced with the opportunity of self-discovery is home. Our response now is to interpret and navigate what we see with a new appreciation and gratitude. When we gaze upon the landscape of our inner being, may we also realize all the strength and courage needed for whatever is next is within us.

When you think of an experience of returning home, when did this happen? What happened when you returned home? Was there something you gave back to those you returned to?

What we learn and accomplish is to be shared. We receive many gifts in life: gifts of necessity and gifts of abundance. When we learn lessons, we are to pass along this wisdom to those seeking to release themselves from the forms and expectations holding them back. Home is also where we practice story-listening.

The greatest life lived brings out the inherent goodness in others. The greatest life looks like a compassionate heart, open mind, and helping hand extending to be a part of another's process of unfolding and refolding. The greatest life is accepting doubt and fear, and stepping into our vulnerability with humility and courage. The greatest life is home.

As OC spoke to YC from the wisdom of Owl: "So, in a world of possibility, why not fly?"

Encouragement and Insight

OC dreamed of becoming a paper plane, or did she dream to fly? A dream that was once hidden has now been discovered. Focusing on where you are at this time; no need to spend too much time on the pain and suffering. No expectation to "treasure hunt" for a reward imagined and of a desire yet to be realized. For in our process, we are discovering where we are at this moment, who is here with us, and what lies within our reach. For here is where our greatest gift awaits.

Our process of unfolding and folding, accepting and risking continues until our last day. One thing we share is that we are all a part of the community of humanity, sharing similar feelings, and reaching for a dream of our most authentic expression of our identity. We are here for each other, and we will fly together. May we try, and may we fly.

Many of us live at the edge of transformation. Having experienced changes, our changes have been left untested. Without testing our changes, we will never know if our transformation is real. Like OC, our platforms in life are the edge of transformation. Here, on our platform and facing the edge is where the voices of shame and guilt, judgment and criticism may sound the loudest. This same place is where our life's new beginning is awaiting.

> Many of us live at the edge of transformation.

> Without testing our changes, we will never know if our transformation is real.

Just as the origami crane in our story dreamed of becoming a paper plane and needed help to transform herself, so too can each one of us benefit from the guidance and support of others to help us transform and reach our full potential. This help can be in the form of personal practices of well-being, a professional coach, mentor, trusted friend, or life partner. The key to transformation is the shaping influence of an outside observer. That special someone who cares, providing an objective observation on our life and dreams.

Like the paper plane that felt a sense of unease in its new form, we may also feel a sense of uncertainty

Reflection and Application

and fear when embarking on a journey of growth and transformation. Our first few efforts at flight, the freedom we seek to express and embody ourselves in a new way, may be awkward. We may question our abilities or worry about leaving our comfort zones. Here is where we need help.

With the right support and practice, we can gain a new perspective on our strengths and weaknesses, identify areas for growth and development, and develop strategies to overcome our fears and achieve our dreams. Transformation is within our reach and it takes time. The great thing is, we do not have to choose between living one way or the other. There is a place where we can find the balance between the person we once were, the person we are today, and the person we are becoming. When we live a life of being alive and free, we find joy and fulfillment in the wholeness of who we are, not in the separation of who we're not.

Who we are today is a delicate balance of being and becoming. Yes, we are both the origami crane and the paper plane. Each form starts with the same raw material: a paper map. We are human beings, individuals seeking to find meaning and purpose through a variety of ways, expressing ourselves in a variety of contexts.

Reflection and Application

Just as OC, in the form of a paper plane, discovered she did not have to choose between her origami crane form and her paper plane form, we will also discover we do not have to fully sacrifice one form

> We do not have to fully sacrifice one form for another. We have the potential for both, just not at the same time.

for another. We have the potential for both, just not at the same time. One form, however, may be more life giving and more promising than another.

OC was transformed by her dream and desire to become a paper plane. We also can be transformed by our dream and desire to grow and reach our full potential. We can chase our dreams to fly. With the support of loved ones and in loving ourselves, we can embrace the process of personal growth and transformation and soar to new heights of meaning and belonging.

Remember, we all start with the same raw material. And who knows, maybe the next form you become is a paper lantern. Let your dream be free.

Reflection and Application

Postlude by Linda

Here's what we know: we are maps. We are people of folds and creases. The maps we are made of point to our nature and identity. Our map is a guidance system reminding us of where we came from and where we are going, providing answers for the challenges we face. We have all had times when we feel tightly and rightly folded, times of unlearning or unfolding, times as an exposed square, and times in a new form.

No one can erase our map. The parts that don't serve us can be tucked away into a fold. The parts that serve us can be put on display. Our shape will continue to evolve as we make peace with the creases and crinkles that help remind us of the people and places of our playgrounds.

We are surrounded by characters. The characters in our life stories shape our lives and our dreams. The acceptance of who we are and the release of greater potential lie in the context of community. That community may not always be filled with champions. Yes, there are wise characters like Owl who provide guidance. There are mature examples like Eagle beckoning us to a better future and reminding us to pay it forward. There are loyal and playful characters like the golden puppy. There are faithful friends with a plan like Turtle and cheerleaders and proteges like YC. There are also characters like Fox and Rabbit. If you're like us, the characters of Rabbit and Fox can amplify any negative self-talk we've already said to ourselves.

We are people on a quest for meaning. As we were folded and placed in the world, our map, folds, playgrounds, friends, and guides shape the folding of our dreams. Self-acceptance doesn't appear the moment we look inside ourselves and get a label from a personality assessment. We need more understanding than just a description, number, color, or letter. The opportunity is to lean into the nuances of what assessments and psychometrics actually point to: our greatest potential.

The more we figure out the clues of who we are and find the courage to fly, the more we will heal ourselves, our families, and communities. This journey is not for the faint of heart.

Unfolded is a mindset as much as it is a practice. A mindset that helps us understand the power of our untapped potential. *Unfolded* gives insights on how to practice the mindset. Many people live their lives without ever experiencing the power of their

Postlude by Linda

potential. In today's society, people are facing the ongoing risk of destabilizing their identity.

> *In today's society, people are facing the ongoing risk of destabilizing their identity.*

The pressures we face on a daily basis include how much time we spend reacting to the opinions, demands, and biases of others, carefully crafting our social identity and caring for our physical and emotional well-being.

In contrast, what would it look like to spend more time understanding our beauty, talents, and potential? How would seeing the best in people change how we live? What if we were on teams where people were cheering for our micro-adaptations and transformation so we can be better humans to each other? We each have the ability to fly, why not try?

For all those who have given us hope and encouragement, thank you. For all those who have challenged us and reminded us we are human, thank you. Go help others live their dreams.

Some dreams we cycle through quickly. Some *Unfolded* moments take us from dream to fly to home in an afternoon before dinner. Some dreams will be cycled over a lifetime. Together we can dream brighter. Together we can face the ups and downs and many days of life. Our hope is you'll try. Our dream is you'll fly.

Postlude by Linda

OC's Meditation (because she gets the last word)

Brian Schubring

Awaken the spark that is within you
Stir your dream from its restful sleep
For this small light is destined to shine bright
And illuminate all that is in and around you
You start with kindness and gentle acceptance
For all of who you are, all you are meant to be

Deep within you there lies a map
A specific and colorful design all your own
Everything you will ever need is found here, in the
contours and landscapes
Your map will guide the way, answer your "why,"
"where," and "with whom"

Now trust in your dream and lean into the process
As challenge will ask you to transform into
something new

You will learn and you will doubt, you will fear and be courageous
And this is all a part of your becoming all you dream to be

And remember those who have brought you here
Those who accept and love, and those who resist and oppose
All are a part of your growing, folding, and molding
For there will come a time, and you will know when this is
To pass along all you have learned, to someone who is longing
To dream the dream that one day they may fly

OC's Meditation (because she gets the last word)

Acknowledgments

The unfolding of the writing of *Unfolded* took place in many figurative playgrounds around the world and with many leaders who have unknowingly shaped and reshaped this book.

We are grateful for the clients who have trusted us over the decades and the countless individuals and teams we have coached. Their commitment to investing in their people and promoting growth has been a sincere source of inspiration. We are honored to have been a part of many stories and journeys in the mountain and valley folds of life. We uncovered more of our vocation in the context of our work with others. Thank you to our clients who held origami cranes made out of maps and helped us find even deeper meaning.

Unfolded was made possible by people who believed in us.

Thank you to the exceptional team at Book Highlight whose hard work, creativity, and commitment have been invaluable, and this accomplishment is a testament to your incredible efforts. A special thanks to Mat Miller, Peter Knox, and Brian Morrison.

We would also like to thank the team at Wiley Publishing; your dedication and expertise have surprised us throughout the process: Zach Schisgal, Amanda Pyne, and Michelle Hacker. And to Dena Young who became a valuable source of confidence and calm for two first-time authors.

Thank you to the creative team at Design Pickle not just for your beautiful illustrations, but for your encouragement and advancing the story: Jon Eddy, Luciana Pugliese, Andrea Vergara, and all the illustrators.

Thank you to artist Kathleen Sheridan, who helped fold our dream into a reality.

A heartfelt thank you to the incredible pre-readers of this manuscript—your thoughtful feedback and invaluable insights shaped the book.

Where would we be without the key relationships that have shaped us in our professional journey? To the mentors, colleagues, and partners who have challenged, supported, and inspired us, we are eternally grateful for the role you have played in shaping our work and perspective. Thank you, Deborah Dixson and Dr. Chip Kimball for the playgrounds and characters you have introduced to us to; for seeing who we really are on the inside and in the space between us; and for believing in us daily. You have both played equal parts Owl and Eagle.

Thank you for the shaping wisdom from Dr. Keith Anderson, Amy Noelle, and David Orbuch.

Thank you, Mercedes Austin. Without your instigation and inspiration, this book would never have taken flight.

Thank you to all the meditation teachers of Insight Timer who have helped us be still, heal, and find inspiration each day.

Thank you to all those who have been part of the many iterations of the Leadership Vision Team over the years. A special thank you to Nathan Freeburg: your friendship, ideas, and brilliance never let us give up. You, Nathan, are the open-armed dad of the playground.

Thank you to Mike O'Keefe, our beloved mentor who left this world too soon. When we would try and think outside the box, he would remind us to, "Think inside the book."

Thank you to our parents who have been cheering us on all along. Thank you to our nephews, Conor and Weston, we are honored to watch you grow and unfold your lives. Thank you to our grand dog, Oliver, who inspired the golden retriever in our story. And thank you to our daughter, Camila, whose fierce determination, global perspective, and big dreams have pushed us to shine brighter and reach further.

And finally, a thank you for the love that has grown in the space between us (Linda and Brian). There is more to be unfolded.

About the Authors

Brian Schubring founded Leadership Vision Consulting in 2000, establishing himself as a pioneering entrepreneur in the behavior-based interpretation and application of assessment tools. With an MA in clinical counseling and a fascination with applied neuroscience, Brian combines deep expertise with a unique ability to connect with individuals personally. His passion lies in guiding people to embrace their individuality and unlock their greatest potential to pursue their dreams. Through consulting and executive coaching, Brian's approach is grounded in attentive listening and thoughtful encouragement, helping clients achieve clarity and confidence in their personal and professional journeys.

Brian's identity is deeply rooted in his passion for athletics and holistic health. Brian established himself as an elite amateur athlete, competing in over 50 marathons, 250 triathlons, and 3 Ironman triathlons. His dedication to promoting healthier living extends from his four-decade commitment as a fitness instructor to the practice of the disciplines of a mystic every morning since he was 17. Brian's commitment to physical and personal growth continues to shape his approach to life and work and inspires others.

Dr. Linda Schubring is the president, owner, and principal consultant of Leadership Vision Consulting, bringing decades of experience in leadership, change, and organizational culture. Linda holds a Doctorate in Intercultural Studies (DIS) from Fuller Graduate School, with research centered on how multinational leaders navigate change in diverse European cultural contexts. She also earned her BA from Bethel University and an MA from Ball State University, blending academic excellence with practical expertise to drive meaningful impact in her work.

As a breast cancer survivor, Linda brings a profound understanding of resilience and the human capacity for growth through adversity. Her journey has deepened her ability to connect with others on an emotional level, creating spaces that are both safe and transformative. Linda's empathy and insight inspire those around her to navigate challenges with courage and find meaningful paths forward.

Together, Linda and Brian create transformative experiences where individuals feel seen, known, and understood. Their company, Leadership Vision Consulting, is a global firm based in Minneapolis, Minnesota, renowned for driving change across organizations of all sizes and industries. From Fortune 100 companies, government agencies, and nonprofits to entrepreneurial startups, universities, and international schools, their work integrates the principles of positive psychology, neuroscience, and adaptive leadership to empower individuals and inspire meaningful organizational transformation.

Dr. Linda and Brian Schubring bring unparalleled expertise to their work, having engaged with over 250,000 individuals across 35 countries. With a decade of dedicated research, they focused on uncovering the critical elements that develop a positive team culture, respect individual identities, and strengthen relational connections between teammates. Their hands-on experience includes working with more than 3,000 teams and conducting over 30,000 one-to-one conversations, each grounded in psychometric and assessment insights. Linda and Brian blend market-shaping expertise with profound emotional intelligence to deliver transformative client experiences.

About the Authors

As keynote speakers and facilitators, Linda and Brian captivate audiences with their engaging, thought-provoking, and authentic style. As podcasters, *The Leadership Vision Podcast*™ started in 2017 and is a weekly show that connects with a global audience, blending insight and inspiration. Whether on stage, on camera, behind a microphone, in the boardroom, or through one-on-one executive coaching, Linda and Brian are dedicated to empowering individuals to achieve emotional well-being and professional engagement to fully embrace their life stories.

About the Authors

Index

Index

Index

Fly with Us

Unfold the next chapter in your life by visiting Schubrings.com to find:

-book resources

-community

-podcasts

-business services

-and more

Having a dream is one thing.
Living that dream is another.

Schubrings.com

DR. LINDA & BRIAN
SCHUBRING